SandCastle™

Sports
By the Numbers

Golf
By the Numbers

Desirée Bussiere

Consulting Editor, Diane Craig, M.A./Reading Specialist

A Division of ABDO

ABDO
Publishing Company

visit us at www.abdopublishing.com

Published by ABDO Publishing Company, a division of ABDO, P.O. Box 398166, Minneapolis, Minnesota 55439. Copyright © 2014 by Abdo Consulting Group, Inc. International copyrights reserved in all countries. No part of this book may be reproduced in any form without written permission from the publisher. SandCastle™ is a trademark and logo of ABDO Publishing Company.

Printed in the United States of America, North Mankato, Minnesota
062013
092013

 PRINTED ON RECYCLED PAPER

Editor: Liz Salzmann
Content Developer: Nancy Tuminelly
Cover and Interior Design and Production: Colleen Dolphin, Mighty Media
Cover Production: Kate Hartman
Photo Credits: Shutterstock, Thinkstock

Library of Congress Cataloging-in-Publication Data

Bussiere, Desiree, 1989-
  Golf by the numbers / Desiree Bussiere.
     pages cm. -- (Sports by the numbers)
  ISBN 978-1-61783-843-9
1. Golf--Juvenile literature. I. Title.
  GV968.B87 2014
  796.352--dc23
                       2012049959

SandCastle™ Level: Transitional

SandCastle™ books are created by a team of professional educators, reading specialists, and content developers around five essential components—phonemic awareness, phonics, vocabulary, text comprehension, and fluency—to assist young readers as they develop reading skills and strategies and increase their general knowledge. All books are written, reviewed, and leveled for guided reading, early reading intervention, and Accelerated Reader® programs for use in shared, guided, and independent reading and writing activities to support a balanced approach to literacy instruction. The SandCastle™ series has four levels that correspond to early literacy development. The levels are provided to help teachers and parents select appropriate books for young readers.

Emerging Readers
(no flags)

Beginning Readers
(1 flag)

Transitional Readers
(2 flags)

Fluent Readers
(3 flags)

Contents

Introduction

Numbers are used all the time in golf.

- A golf **course** has either 9 or 18 holes.

- There are 5 kinds of golf clubs. They are irons, woods, hybrids, chippers, and putters.

- There are 3 basic kinds of golf strokes. They are **drive**, **chip**, and **putt**.

- A hole can have a par of 3, 4, 5, or 6.

- A **standard** golf tee is 2⅛ inches (5.4 cm) long.

Let's learn more about how numbers are used in golf.

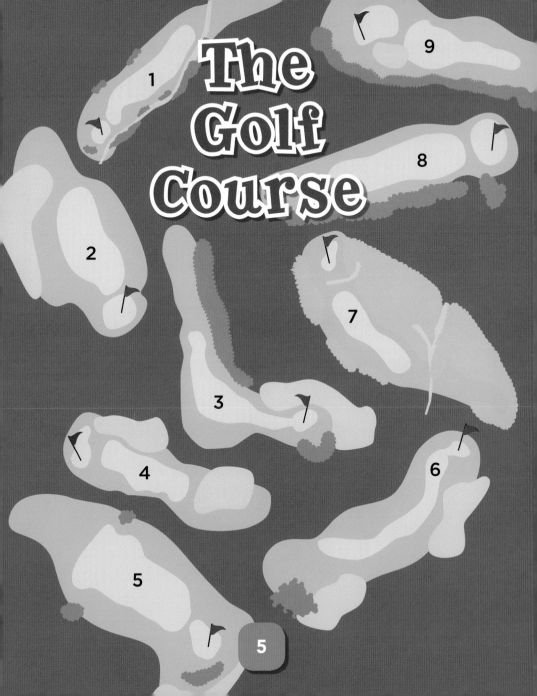

The Golf Course

The Sport

Each hole starts at the tee box.

The golfer hits the ball until it goes in the hole.

Each hit equals 1 stroke.

The person with the fewest strokes wins.

Par is how many strokes it should take to finish the hole. It is based on how far the hole is from the tee box.

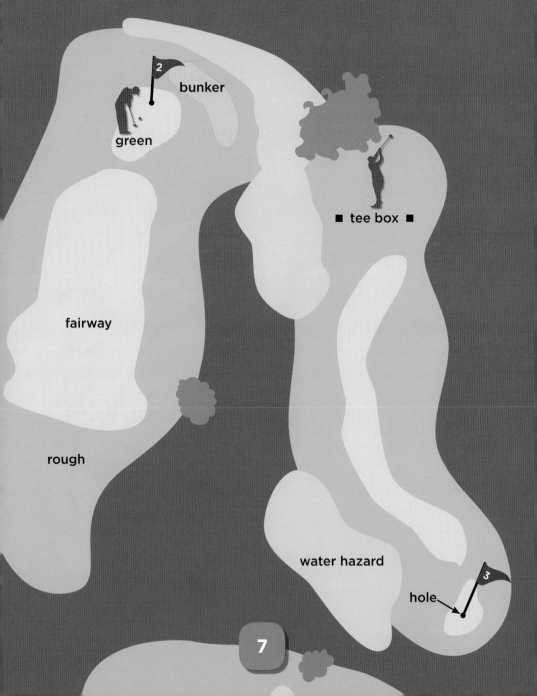

bunker

2

green

fairway

rough

tee box ■

water hazard

hole

3

7

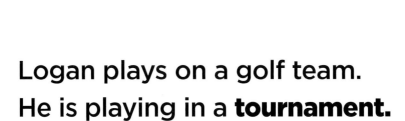

Logan plays on a golf team.
He is playing in a **tournament.**

By the Numbers!

Ⓐ

There are 7 tournaments each year. Logan's team
has played in 6. How many more are there?

(answer on p. 23)

9

10

Ashley is on the green. She **putted** the ball toward the hole.

B

It took Ashley 6 strokes to get to the green. She putted it 2 times on the green. How many total times did she hit the ball?

(answer on p. 23)

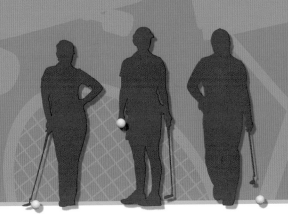

Cody goes golfing with his dad.

By the Numbers!

C Cody is 10 years old. Cody's dad started teaching him to golf 3 years ago. How old was he when he first played golf?

(answer on p. 23)

14

Brian practices his swing at a **driving** range.

By the Numbers!

Brian practiced 2 days last week. He practiced 1 day this week. How many days has he practiced?

(answer on p. 23)

15

Jason's ball is near the hole. Jason uses his putter.

By the Numbers!

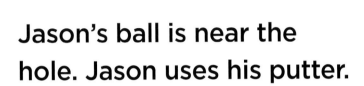

E The hole is a par 5. Jason has hit the ball 4 times. How many more strokes can he take and still make par?

(answer on p. 23)

18

Missy plays on a 9-hole **course** with her family.

By the Numbers!

F

The course has 9 holes. Missy has played 7 of them. How many holes are left?

(answer on p. 23)

20

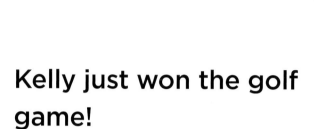

Kelly just won the golf game!

By the Numbers!

G

Kelly made par on 4 holes. She was over par on 5 holes. How many holes did she play?

(answer on p. 23)

Golf Facts

- There are 336 dimples on a golf ball.

- Arnold Palmer is a famous golfer. He has won more than 90 **tournaments**.

- People love golf. It's been played for more than 500 years.

- There are about 16,000 golf **courses** in the United States.

- The longest golf **drive** was 515 yards (471 m). Mike Austin hit it in 1974.

Answers to By the Numbers!

D

$$\begin{array}{r} 2 \\ +1 \\ \hline 3 \end{array}$$

Brian practiced 2 days last week. He practiced 1 day this week. How many days has he practiced?

A

$$\begin{array}{r} 7 \\ -6 \\ \hline 1 \end{array}$$

There are 7 **tournaments** each year. Logan's team has played in 6. How many more are there?

E

$$\begin{array}{r} 5 \\ -4 \\ \hline 1 \end{array}$$

The hole is a par 5. Jason has hit the ball 4 times. How many more strokes can he take and still make par?

B

$$\begin{array}{r} 6 \\ +2 \\ \hline 8 \end{array}$$

It took Ashley 6 strokes to get to the green. She **putted** it 2 times on the green. How many total times did she hit the ball?

F

$$\begin{array}{r} 9 \\ -7 \\ \hline 2 \end{array}$$

The **course** has 9 holes. Missy has played 7 of them. How many holes are left?

C

$$\begin{array}{r} 10 \\ -3 \\ \hline 7 \end{array}$$

Cody is 10 years old. Cody's dad started teaching him to golf 3 years ago. How old was he when he first played golf?

G

$$\begin{array}{r} 4 \\ +5 \\ \hline 9 \end{array}$$

Kelly made par on 4 holes. She was over par on 5 holes. How many holes did she play?

Glossary

chip – to hit a golf ball a short distance in the air.

course – an area where golf is played.

drive – to hit a golf ball a long distance in the air.

putt – to hit a golf ball a short distance on the ground.

standard – most often used.

tournament – a series of contests or games played to win a championship.